INNER NATU1

MW00804176

A Carl Jung Coloring Book for Self-Exploration

By Annette Poizner, MSW, Ed.D., RSW

INNER NATURE: THE CARL JUNG COLORING BOOK FOR SELF-EXPLORATION COPYRIGHT © 2021 BY ANNETTE POIZNER. ALL RIGHTS RESERVED.

"Thus all the past is abandoned: for one day the herd might become master and drown all time in shallow waters. Therefore, O my brothers, a new nobility is needed to be the adversary of all mob rule and despotism and to write again the word 'noble' on new tablets."

Nietzsche, *Thus Spoke Zarathustra*

THIS BOOK BELONGS TO ME,

_____

(A WORK IN PROGRESS)

Why would a person spend time coloring? Studies have shown: coloring has therapeutic effects. Additionally, this medium is an untapped teaching tool. We have what to learn, and master, if we will use this modality. Further, coloring books can be used to teach content, important lessons about self, life, identity and more.

In Volume 1, we explored some of Dr. Carl Jung's ideas. In this volume, we will consider archetypes and myths, but use a novel means of exploring the archetypes; doing so with the aid of the animal kingdom. First, though, more on coloring.

LEARNING HOW TO SEE

In different ways, we are oblivious to reality. For example, we are naive to nuance. We rush around and lose awareness, say, of the magnificently intricate patterns in nature. Take the following example: you look up from the computer and see the tree outside. You don't process the collage of leaves, layers of texture, the color palettes. You just see 'tree'.

Many adult coloring books bring awareness to the complex repeating patterns in the world around us. These books often emphasize and exaggerate detail. Gertrude Stein said: " I like to go to museums. I like to go to museums so I can look out the window." Coloring books, similarly, let us 'look out the window'.

They encourage a type of detailed apprehension that goes beyond that of everyday life while reminding us that there is more detail that we could access. We can come to appreciate all there is to see!!

Now there's another way we are fooled by reality. Your perceptual systems represent the world as coherent and organized. You recognize the objects around you, the people, the sounds. Is reality really that orderly, though? It isn't. You are only perceiving a thin band of the present.

You sit under a tree at the nearby park. Say you're in a quiet, contemplative mood. The weather is pleasant. The view is peaceful. There is this quality of stillness although you are aware of background sounds. Are you fully registering the reality of the moment? What aren't you seeing?

You're not seeing the buzz of insects that are ensconced in their busyness right near you. If children are playing in the distance, you hear them but you're not seeing the actual soundwaves which carry the sounds. For that matter, you're not seeing other waves that are similarly invisible to the human eye. You know that in the homes nearby there are televisions, telephones, radios, computers, all receiving data. If you could consciously perceive the various frequencies streaming above you and around you, the scene would probably be quite busy. My point here is that reality, in

reality, is complex, multi-faceted and chaotic. We are spared a good deal of information.

Some adult coloring books bring us to a realization about reality. They remind us that we live amidst infinite detail and complexity. They emphasize that complexity, requiring us to commune with it, versus tune it out.

Along those lines, coloring books require us to patiently invest in an activity that requires fidelity to detail. The activity pays off to the degree that you focus single-mindedly on each small segment. The activity and its impressive product, when it is well done, is a lesson we can easily generalize to life itself. "Imagine if I put that much intention, care and follow-through into all my activities!" How many of your outcomes would be that much better, if you did everything to the standard that you use when working on an adult coloring book.

We are going to see that working with a coloring book will help deliver content that relates to the self as it processes a complex reality and simultaneously offers a process that, itself, is both instructive and therapeutic. You will also see that there is another layer of learning and reflection that occurs when we think about ideas and process them using visual media. Visual images give us another way of unpacking ideas.

Further, thinking about quotes shared by Dr. Carl Jung, we are going to learn about reality, about the Self and the challenges of bringing that self to fruition. But first, you might want to grab some gel pens and get to work!

In the first volume of the series, *The Moon and the Man: A Carl Jung Coloring Book for Self-Exploration*, I presented Jung's model of the psyche as well as images that conceptually represent the Self, which is a composite of all the constituent parts of the psyche. In this volume, we undertake a growth exercise in keeping with Jung's challenge that each person identify the myth he or she lives out.

Of course, these days, we do not study the myths of yesteryear. In this volume, then, I propose that we explore the various archetypes as they are expressed in different animals we find in the animal kingdom. Each animal is characterized by traits and habits that, interestingly, can inform self-insight and guide us in our individuation process.

Find your animal, the one that guides you! Then identify the animals that teach lessons and lifestyles that you could well use as you develop yourself in new and interesting ways. And get out your markers! It's time to color in or, more specifically, time to color Yin, as per Chinese medicine, pun intended! The Yin dimension takes you to your essence and relates to aspects of self that are archaic and unconscious, much like the animals as they relate to your unique proclivities and constitution.

While you are coloring and processing the different archetypes, make special notice of the dreams you wake up with. Carl Jung, in his approach to psychology, underscored the importance of dreams. The second part of this book is a dream journal. As you color and process the animals, taking stock of the archetypes they represent, your unconscious mind will process further when you dream at night. Record the dreams. See if you can learn even more about who you are, at essence, and who you could be, with a little more conscious intention!

"...the sole purpose of human existence is to kindle a light in the darkness of mere being."
— Carl Jung

"At times I feel as if I am spread out over the landscape and inside things, and am myself living in every tree, in the splashing of the waves, in the clouds and the animals that come and go, in the procession of the seasons. There is nothing in the Tower that has not grown into its own form over the decades, nothing with which I am not linked. Here everything has its history, and mine; here is space for the spaceless kingdom of the world's and the psyche's hinterland."
Carl Jung

IN THE BEGINNING

Let's start at a beginning. May I take you to a statement in the Genesis account of creation? Prior to creating man, there is a line we read: "Let *us* make man," Who, exactly, is this 'us'?

According to commentators, 'us' refers: to all of creation. Every part of creation will have a hand in creating Man, Therefore, humans find within all the elements, all the animals, the luminaries . . . Everything!

But is it so?

We find mineral, water, air and even fire (electrical charge? hot blood?) within the human body. Do we find the luminaries? Let's think of the conscious self as the Sun; the unconscious, as the Moon. But what about the animals? Do we find the animals within?

Many traditions do. For one thing, Judaism posits that each person has an 'animal soul', a part of the self that operates on a more instinctual level. If not governed properly, this part fuels addictions and compulsions. If properly governed/ integrated, this part undertakes the physical aspects of existence but does so in a way that is modulated and useful.

Certainly, in the Native tradition, animals play a role in our psychology; each person has a specific guide from nature, a specific animal that relates to each one's idiosyncratic nature. Tha t animal, in some way, 'accompanies' him or her throughout life. The person might have an affinity for that particular animal, or may have similarities, character traits or other patterns that correspond to that animal.

Certainly astrological systems correlate particular astrological signs with specific animals and their traits. In fact, Chinese astrology uses the traits of various animals to designate different personality types.

Think about another fact: it is not uncommon to describe people using language that relates to animals. We might say that someone eats like a bird or describe someone as an angry bear. Maybe we use descriptive words that relate to the animal world: "cold-blooded," "parasitic," "nocturnal," "man-eating," "spineless," "wild," etc. Does this language imply that we find the animals, in one sense or another, within?

I will suggest that, as per Genesis, we find within the traits of all the animals; they function like archetypes that guide us and give us a frame of reference for thinking about ourselves and others. You likely have one animal that resonates with your calling.

Are you a workhorse? A busy bee? A proud peacock? A wise owl? Are you a spider, a homebody who possesses a sixth sense? Are you a lion, nocturnal, with a big, social personality? ? A loyal dog? An independent cat? A playful monkey? A busy beaver? Do you scurry about like a squirrel? Lumber like an elephant? Are you a stubborn goat?

Do you have affinities for certain animals? A penchant for butterflies?

As you color the animals in this book, see if certain animals remind you of your lifestyle, sensibility or pace. Or, conversely, consider whether these animals have traits that you might want to cultivate. Also: as you proceed, thinking of the traits and associations to any given animal, think of friends and relatives. Do you know people who remind you of specific animals, as per the descriptions mentioned? The animals give us an interesting lens for thinking about the personalities of people we know.

YOUR 'LETTER'

Before looking at the animals, let's return to Genesis. Some commentators read the first line of that book in an interesting way. Instead of processing the whole sentence about Heaven and Earth fully, some prefer to analyze the first four words to decipher an idea carefully encoded within those words. Read that way, you would translate those four Hebrew words in the following way: "In the beginning, G-d created the Aleph Beit" (that being the Hebrew alphabet).

The fourth word of Genesis is a word that technically doesn't have an independent meaning: it is comprised of the first and the last letter of the Hebrew alphabet. Therefore, the Bible hints that before actually creating the Heavens and the Earth, the Hebrew alphabet was created. If

the world is created by speech, it would follow that language would be amongst the very first of the creations. Were that true: the Hebrew letters could be thought of as the DNA of Creation, the DNA of the world.

Now one more idea: Rabbi Tsadok HaCohen suggested that just as there are 600,000 letters of the Torah, so, too, are there 600,000 root souls that constitute the Jewish people. Each person in that community, then, embodies one of the letters in the Torah or a part of one of the letters. The real Torah, he, therefore, asserts, is the 'Torah of souls'.

He writes:

"Just as there is a scroll of ink on parchment, so is there a scroll of souls that includes the entire unfolding of generations. The sum total of the soul-sparks of the Jewish people comprise a single and complete Torah... The real Torah.... Yet this scroll of souls is virtually impossible to read. It's lights are too bright and too complex for the human mind to fathom, at least at its earlier stages of development.

And so, the Torah of ink on parchment serves as its commentary, presenting the same teachings in a more condensed and readable format. In our immaturity, we don't see that the commentary is only an aide to enable our access to the real Torah, the Torah of souls. But, as we grow and mature and move toward perfection, we come to see things more from G-d's perspective which assigns priority to the people whose souls are actually the inner lights of the Torah.... The whole point is to learn to read the living Torah that shines through each person as he or she dances out the teaching of the letter that is the root of his or her soul..."

I share this idea to suggest that each person - Jew or non-Jew - has a unique essence, a unique and specific role in the world; each is a puzzle piece that fits into the cosmic puzzle of humanity if only he or she will figure out who each needs to be to properly fit and do the job that is his or hers. You could say, we are each a specific Hebrew letter of the Torah. But, arguably, it might be easier to consider the archetypes by seeing how they play out in the animal kingdom, than studying the Hebrew letters to determine how the same archetypes are at play.

Next, then, we will consider ourselves relative to the nature, proclivities, talents and 'ways' of different animals. You will look to see whether one animal calls to you. Are you introverted like a cat? Extroverted like a dog? Of course, we are - and should be - multifaceted. If we are to more fully develop ourselves, we want to find ALL the animals within. We can, then, think of ourselves in terms of the animals. Nature provides us with an interesting language for thinking about personality.

The exercises that follow have been developed by Dr. Meshulom Teller to help psychotherapy clients ponder identity and identify areas for personal development. I

include these exercises alongside the coloring task, allowing readers to self-explore: "what character traits have I mastered and which might I work on cultivating as a next step?"

Can we think of ourselves and others in our universe using this interesting lens? Can it help us to imagine that all the animals and their unique and idiosyncratic natures are 'onboard' and we merely have to find them within? Can the language of creation help us bring ourselves to fruition so that we come to a place that we do, indeed, find the universe within? Let's see what can be achieved. And as you color each animal, contemplate ways you can or do channel that animal in your day-to-day life!

SOMETHING TO TRY . . .

Imagine yourself at work or doing a typical activity. If you conceived your job/task, imagining yourself as an animal doing what you do in the course of an average day, what animal would you be? The detailed protocol of a worker bee? Providing support and care like a mother hen? The work ethic and service of a horse? Imagine your colleagues as animals. What would they be? Similarly, come up with an animal that meaningfully corresponds to your friends, your partner, your kids.

Now, here is the 'family of origin' version of this exercise. Imagine your parents, each as an animal. Which animal corresponds to the overall personality style of each. Once you come up with animals, now check and see if it works. See if you can imagine the dynamic of their relationship using the patterns associated with the animals. Is mom tending to dad like a mother hen while dad withdraws like an owl?

Once you get their dynamic down using the language of the animals, think about your siblings. Can you come up with an animal for each? Can you imagine each of their animals interacting with the animals you came up with for the parents?

Now, come up with an animal that captures your way of being in the context of the family. You get the drift . . .

Once you have come up with animals that relate to your core patterns, imagine if you were to extend yourself, taking on new ways of being. If you were to roll out new interests, new ways of relating, which animal would you need to emulate? Imagine channeling elephant, different than, say, the workhorse that resonates easily. How could you find more diversity within, stretching into new ways of being? This is an exercise that allows you to imagine and conceptualize new traits, new patterns, new possible identities.

With that as an introduction, I'd like to share some ideas about the various animals, discussing the signature traits of each. To use this gallery for self-insight, you might journal about each animal that you color.

In assembling comments about the signature traits of each animal, I have surveyed interesting facts about each species and also explored wisdom from ancient traditions or even modern day sources which ascribe certain traits to those animals. My assumption is that, over the centuries, we have come up with insights about animals which have found their way into folklore or fairytales and we can consult those sources to garner insight into the inner nature of each species. Of course, what I have assembled here is preliminary. One could do a much more thorough investigation into the patterns of any given animal. I encourage readers to explore further, looking at other sources, to supplement the insights that I present here.

THE GALLERY

THE BEE

Bees, as a species, are extremely organized and communal. In any given colony, there will be thousands of worker bees, each partaking a specific job obediently, carefully and in perfect sync with the others. When the bee is your archetype, you may be here to devote yourself to the collective good and work within systems. Your mentality may be that of the faithful servant, devoid of ego, tireless, with visions of progress that you realize alongside others. If you tend to be the isolate, working on your own page and your own page only, you may need to animate this archetype in order to awaken your desire to be of service to the broader community.

Meredith May wrote *The Honey Bus: A Memoir of Loss, Courage and a Girl Saved by Bees*. In this wonderful book, the author describes her dysfunctional family and how she learned life lessons about harmonious living from the bees and from her grandfather, a beekeeper. In other words, for this woman, the archetype of the bee literally saved her life. To this day she is a journalist . . . and a beekeeper.

THE BUTTERFLY

Butterflies fly in an erratic way which helps them avoid predators. In fact, butterflies are 'erratic' in other ways.. Who would otherwise expect a lowly caterpillar to morph into a butterfly? The butterfly represents the alchemical process whereby something can mutate into something much greater, against all odds and without our full understanding how this transformation is even possible. The butterfly also reminds us that to bring our goals to fruition we undergo a range of developmental stages. The butterfly would have us be patient with the various stages of development that we (and others) will undergo.. Know that the caterpillar is going to evolve into something else, something better! Patience is key!

If the butterfly is your archetype, watch for the pitfall: being a social butterfly who flutters here and there, then quickly flits off somewhere else. Once transformed, be sure to drop roots and make lasting commitments. Each species can teach us virtues or vices! We must master the former and limit the latter!

THE PEACOCK

The male peacock, known for its beautiful plume, was a pet amongst royalty who would let the bird loose on grand estates as a decorative feature. Once placed there, and with all needs met, the peacock would live a staid existence, a happy showpiece not inclined to leave since all amenities were provided. The peacock may signify your personal expression at its best. Perhaps this animal is the forbearer of the luxury goods industry! If you're going to produce it, make it exceptional!

Here's another interesting fact: peacocks eat snakes. Snakes, as per the Garden of Eden, symbolize the shadow, the negativity within. Jung would say that if we confront and transform our shadow, we actualize the hidden potential within. The peacock may represent that optimal yield, reminding us how we look when we shine our light unfettered by the shadow, once it has been neutralized or deconstructed.

THE FISH

The Jewish tradition likens the soul to a fish, egoless, unaware of the status of self and most comfortable assuming a humble and quiet place within the 'school' of fish. The Hebrew Bible accords special status to the fish. One reason? Because in the flood story of Genesis, all the wildlife of that time had been corrupted and were participating in intra-species relations. The fish were the only life form that had retained purity. Legend reports that they were, therefore, not destroyed by the flood.

When you animate this archetype you are simple, humble, obedient and selfless. Fish remind us each of our small – but important – place in the world. They also remind us that we only thrive in a state of purity and, therefore, require us to review our influences so as to ensure high standards and to avoid toxicity. What are you looking at in movies, on TV, on social media? What are you ingesting?

Channel this archetype and, minus ego, you'll find yourself more adaptable and able to go with the flow; less moody, more accepting; less rigid, more able to accommodate. In Chinese culture, fish are a sign of good fortune and financial prosperity. Some Chinese people keep fish in their home to attract this good luck. The fish is an avatar for humility and this is a psychological stance that is venerated in Chinese culture.

"Like the sea itself, the unconscious yields an endless and self-replenishing abundance of creatures, a wealth beyond our fathoming."

Carl Jung

THE CAT

House cats are characterized by a self-possessed, independent nature. They slink silently, easily avoiding detection, and are prone to hiding in out-of-the-way, hard-to-find spots. This tendency to retract or pull back – to maintain separateness – may add to the allure of the domestic cat. Cat owners enjoy the bond they have with their cat; once trust has been won, there is a feeling of exclusivity. The devotion of the cat is appreciated all the more because of the initial phase of aloofness.

The cat may represent a capacity we can each cultivate: to be self-possessed, confident, prioritizing self when this is necessary and functioning as an independent who, over time, attracts admirers. If you are prone to lose yourself, pandering to others, channeling the house cat helps you prioritize your self-importance.

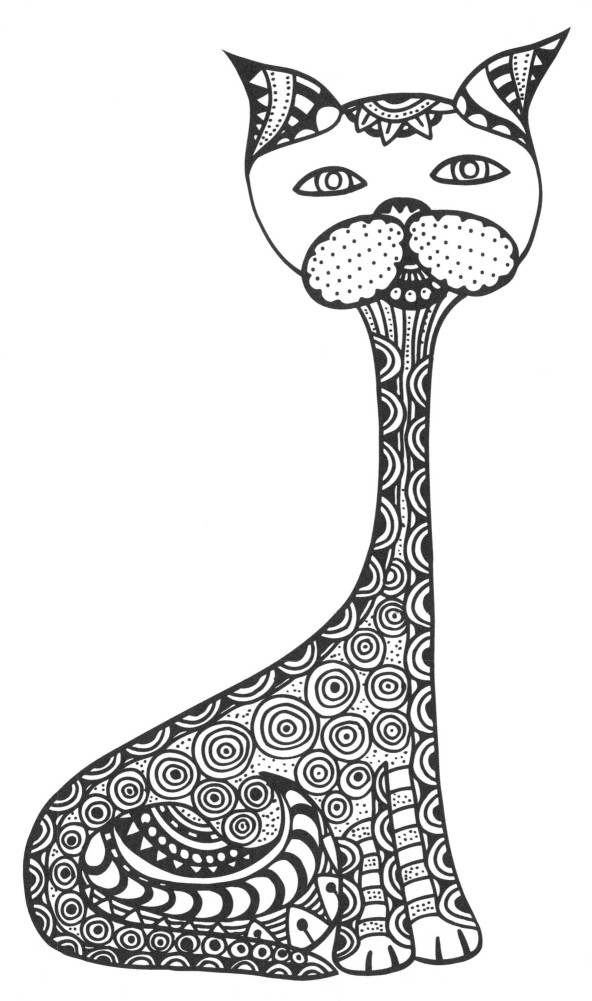

23

THE DOG

In Hebrew, the name for dog is *kelev* which has a meaning: "like a heart." The dog is bighearted, accounting for its affectionate, loyal, enthusiastic, extroverted nature and its willingness to serve the master.

THE PARROT

Parrots are the superstars of the animal kingdom. When you are due to knock it out of the ballpark, you might take inspiration from your local parrot!

Parrots are amongst the most intelligent birds. Many can use tools and solve problems. Monogamous, they pair for life, a rather impressive accomplishment compared to similar efforts in our species! They have no lips, no teeth and no vocal cords, yet they can make sounds that humans cannot, partly because they are able to breathe and simultaneously make a sound. Humans can't do both at once.

According to the Guinness Book of World Records, the parrot who had the largest vocabulary was Puff the Parrot who knew more than 1700 words! Parrots are striking in virtually every way. When they sleep, they do so standing on one leg! Most have dramatic colorful feathers. They are the only bird that eats with their feet! They have a desire to communicate which prompts them to mimic sounds – to effectively sing your song when they live with you – and they imitate words and voice tones better than most people can.

We channel the parrot when we wear bright colors and when we do any kind of head-turning performance, when we step up to the plate, cultivating exemplary skills and achieve an accomplishment that is – hands down – impressive.

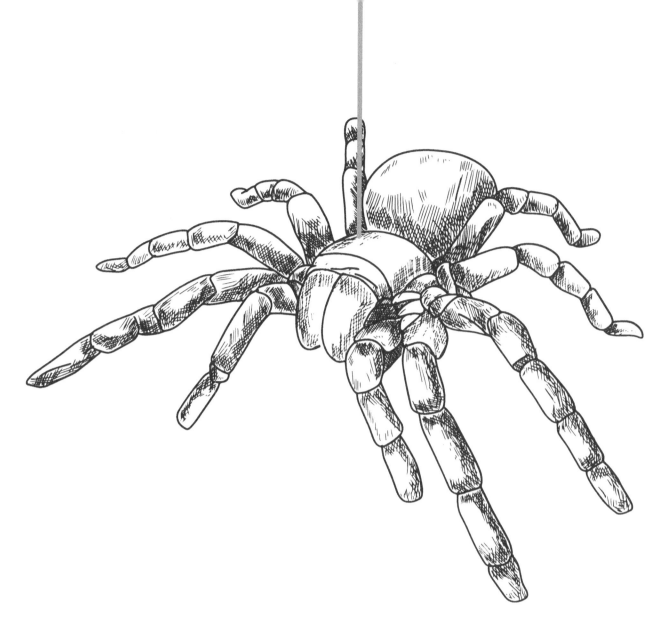

THE SPIDER

Spiders are unique creatures. Living in the center of the web they spin, some sacred traditions understand the spider as metaphorically symbolizing the Creator, hidden in in the center of His creation. The spider is the penultimate creative, perhaps representing the individual with talents to manifest, also the independent spirit who thrives in his or her own company. Ever notice that the artistic temperament is sometimes manifest in the individual with a thin, frail, weak body? And sometimes very nearsighted, with poor vision like the spider! These types are sometimes fragile, sensitive, easily crushed, like the spider!

As well, spiders cannot digest solid food. They liquefy their food. If spider is your archetype, you may be sensitive to what you eat. On the other hand, spiders rely on vibration to navigate and find their prey. Humans might call that inner knowing or intuition. Again, we are describing the artistic, sensitive temperament.

The spider is a predator. Expect an intensity, a decided thrust when pursuing its goals. All these traits can be manifest by those who channel spider, and doing so can have them using their artistic gifts to spin their web, making their own little universe in which they can live and invent.

THE REPTILE

You've probably heard that part of the human brain has been called the reptilian brain. The brainstem and the cerebellum are parts of the brain that are similarly found in the reptile's brain. This part of the brain controls basic vital functions: heart rate, breathing, body temperature and balance, amongst others. It also governs primitive drives such as thirst, hunger, sexuality and territoriality. With regards to the latter, this part of the brain motivates our desire to dominate and is prone to rigidity. When you lapse into 'us versus them' thinking, you may be exerting the inner reptile. On the other hand, if you've endured trauma and are prone to strong 'fight or flight' reactions, you might need some other influences to help soften these reactions and to get out of a pattern which floods you with cortisol, the stress hormone.

THE HORSE

Horses are useful and reliable workers. They represent the work ethic we can animate bringing projects to fruition by applying strength and obedience. They allow us to get outcomes way beyond our normal capacities. Channel the horse if you want to add horsepower to your project.

Horses like carrots and we have an expression where we refer to the act of providing incentives as giving a carrot. If the horse represents something of our animal strength, we understand that we need to incentive ourselves to motivate our best performance. We can catalyze the 'inner horse' and get projects moving. What healthy treat can you give yourself so as to reward (and ensure) your maintenance of a good work ethic?

Another association to the horse is the wild mustang: chaotic and rebellious. It is our task to domesticate the horse within, not using brutal measures, but to have a good working relationship which ensures a healthy lifestyle and successful outcomes. Note that horse consciousness is non-predatory thinking. Horses live in herds. The horse within is prosocial and has good 'horse sense'.

THE ANT

From ants we learn alacrity, team ship, preplanning and allegiance to the group agenda. Ants are not lazy! They do their job without any one ant being in the alpha leadership position. They plan for the future. They spend much time gathering food to store underground which will see them through the winter. They live communally and work in a coordinated way, each ant egoless, obediently serving the priority of the group. Mobilize the ant when there's a job to get done and when you need to get past the politics and personalities in order to get the job done!

THE LION

With a large, muscular body and males that have a dramatic mane, lions have a strong presence, with looks that attract mates and discourage power grabs by other males. Unlike all the other felines, lions are highly social. They live with other lions in a grouping called a pride. The males have strong leadership skills, making decisions and delegating the hunt to the female lions who will work collectively to bring in prey to feed the pride. Lions, known as the king of the jungle, begin verbalizing when very young and ultimately master their roar, loud and dramatic. Channel the lion when it's time to animate status and command respect and admiration. Lion is your go to when you are coming out of your shell and coming into a place of prominence relative to the social world around you. Time to shine your light.

THE WOLF

To understand the signature traits of the wolf, you can think of some of our English expressions that relate to wolves: "to wolf down your food," "to keep the wolf from the door," "to keep the wolves at bay," "to throw someone to the wolves," "a wolf in sheep's clothing."

Carnivores, wolves have heavy and large teeth that can crush bones. They are characterized by power and massive strength. They tend to travel in nuclear families, mated pairs and their offspring. They hunt as a group and, doing so, can take down large game. The pack is governed by a dominant male and they are territorial; they will aggress against trespassing wolves.

If you were to describe wolves in terms that we apply to people, you might describe them as high testosterone. Therefore, somebody who has a shy and introverted nature could probably benefit from channeling wolf energy, whereas too much of this energy may look like unmodulated aggressive tendencies.

THE FOX

Foxes appear in fairytales around the world and are known for their signature trait: cleverness and cunning, as well as mental and physical agility. Beyond their exceptional hearing and detection skills – they can hear mice moving within the snow several feet below them – they are also known to confuse predators by altering their tracks or otherwise hiding to deliberately mislead them. As a result, they have been referred to as tricksters. Another expression of intelligence: they navigate by detecting the magnetic field which helps them hunt successfully.

When foxes attack their prey, they leap, taking decisive action quickly and effectively. If the fox is your archetype, you are strategic, strong, clever . . . and effective!

THE BIRD

Chinese wisdom can help us understand the symbolic meaning of birds. In Traditional Chinese Medicine, the 'Wild Birds of Shen' is the metaphor used to speak about the higher soul, an ethereal part of the self that religious traditions would probably refer to as the Divine Spark. This is an aspect of self that, when it lands, allows us to experience transcendence. Chinese medicine would tell us that when a person properly individuates, the 'Wild Birds of Shen' settle within the chest area, taking up residence. The result: more peacefulness, more clarity, more synchronicity. Our task is to draw down this higher self by living a life of virtue. Speaking of virtue, birds of various species partner for life, unlike many mammals (and people!). Living a life of fidelity to higher principles has us channeling this archetype, and, in so doing, we transcend, rising above worries, accessing a higher, lighter perspective to life – a Birdseye view. Also, conceivably, other benefits: special states of higher consciousness and revelations ('aha' moments).

THE DEER

Deers are perceived as gentle and graceful animals. They are characterized by slim, trim bodies and, as such, are ill-equipped to fight with predators, of which they have many. There signature trait, though, is the ability to flee and the ability to move quickly, gracefully and with much coordination. The secret to the deers success is skittishness. The deer is always alert to its surrounding, at times sleeping with one eye open and, at times, sleeping while standing, ever ready to flee. When necessary, that deer leaps away suddenly. If it's antlers get locked in a tree, the deer will break off an antler in order to escape. Perhaps we channel the deer when we need to live life on the defensive. Those who get in unnecessary tussles with adversaries could learn a thing or two from the deer. This archetype might be useful particularly when we need to be extra vigilant about risk and avoid altercations with those who have predatory intent. Deers help us master the elegant escape!

45

THE OWL

In marketing material, we frequently see owls represented with glasses or even holding a book. Why has the owl become associated with wisdom?

Owls have excellent hearing, excellent night vision and huge round eyes that don't move in their sockets. To compensate for their ocular limitations, their necks swivel. Owls are reclusive and active at night. By day, the owl watches and represents the possession of keen observation skills. The owl, then, personifies the watchful elder, the one who observes by day and only executes a hunt later, having collected all relevant information about the environment via focused observation. Owls live in close proximity to where they were born. They are staid and settled. In Chinese culture, the elder associates with the center point, not the periphery of the wheel. As the wheel turns, there is a lot of action on the periphery. The elder, situated in the center, is all-knowing, less reactive, and experiences less turbulence.

In a society where people are too 'Yang', frenetically doing, engaged in a diffuse type of perception that distracts and compromises attentiveness, this archetype steps forward to encourage stillness and thoughtful observation.

THE SQUIRREL

In English, we talk about a person who squirrels things away. Squirrels bury seeds which they may dig up later, as needed. The energy of the squirrel is frenetic and acrobatic. They run in the zigzag pattern to escape predators. The squirrel seems characterized by nervous frenetic energy, planning for the future, always anticipating needs or risks. By planting those seeds, they end up participating in agricultural agendas, an important part of the growth process. Squirrels are forward thinking! If you need to plan for the future, channel the squirrel! And if you're light on your feet, a movement junkie, always on the run, thinking five steps ahead, fast talking and fast thinking, you may be channeling what the squirrel is here to teach.

THE TURTLE

Cold-blooded, turtles do not interact with other turtles. They plod along, migrate long distances, slowly and with persistence. They are known to have great longevity. They retract into their proverbial shell as necessary and so are self-protective. Remember The Tortoise and the Hare? Slow and steady wins the race! And the turtle helps you channel self-reliance!

THE EAGLE

Eagles have something in common with lions. Both are known as the King of their respective realms. Further, in Scripture, the Creator likens Himself to one or the other. The Eagle, then, is an 'alpha' bird. We can expect characteristics which we should admire and emulate.

Remember the word 'eagle-eyed'? Eagles have strong eyesight and long-distance focus. They hone in on prey and maintain that visual focus until the prey is captured. The Eagle, then, thinks long-range and stays on track till the task is complete. Never lazy, Eagles do not scavenge and will not eat meat that has been killed by other predators. They function as independents.

Many birds take shelter in storms. The Eagle, in contrast, flies into the storm and uses the storm winds to lift itself higher, allowing it to glide and so rest its wings. This tendency could be seen as a willingness to move towards, and not away, from challenges.

When it comes to parenting, Eagles take a 'tough love' approach. Once the eaglets achieve a certain degree of maturity, the Eagles remove the soft feathers from the nests to encourage them to leave. It also lifts the eaglets and drops them out of the nest, pushing them to develop flight skills.

When Eagles are older they will have difficulty flying at the same high heights that they had achieved in youth. Then what they do is remarkable. They fly to the mountains and undergo a process, plucking out weak feathers and claws; they remain in place, effectively hiding, until new feathers and claws grow in. This death-rebirth process might be a lesson for us: what we can achieve if we will shed our old ways and pursue improvement in a dedicated way, this in our older years.

53

THE ELEPHANT

If the wolf is our 'high testosterone' animal, perhaps the elephant may be the feminine counterpart. These large, powerful animals live in packs that are led by females. They are strongly social and communal with a 'family first' mentality. They are loyal, protecting the elders and the babies, highly attuned to the needs of the weak. They use physical contact to be affectionate, are known to experience grief, undertake burial rituals and even have the capacity to mimic human voices. They have also been known to recognize their names. In one interesting demonstration of the elephant's inner nature, an elephant was being guided where to put a log. The elephant was coached and directed to put a log in a hole where a dog was sleeping. The elephant would not do it.

The signature traits of elephants: they are relational, characterized by their devotion and connection; they are strong *and* protective. They remember relationships. We hear stories about elephants that reconnect many years later when they are retired from circuses, reunited with other elephants they have known. They recognize each other and respond warmly!

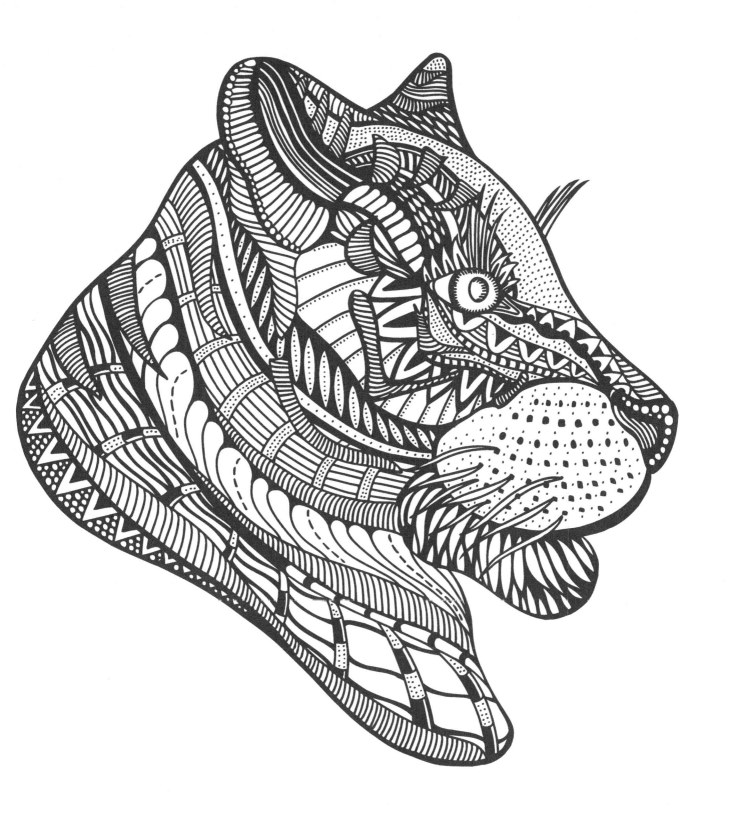

THE COUGAR

The cougar moves quickly, running at a speed of 80 km an hour. It can leap 40 feet horizontally and is known for that signature trait. It is a focused, decisive hunter and may signify the ability of a person to move forward without hesitation, having decided where to head. The cougar, a solitary animal, is the one to channel when you know where to aim and it's now time to act. Also when you're preparing to go it alone, as needed.

THE TIGER

Chinese astrology attributes certain characteristics to people whose birth year associates to the Tiger (as per their system): intense, determined, imaginative, talented. Why these associations?

Tigers are the largest and strongest felines, but they are characterized by their many talents: good swimmers, they have sharp hearing, a strong sense of smell, incredible upper body strength, a tongue with sharp protrusions that can rip off skin and a roar which paralyzes prey.

Tigers live in solitude. If you need to bring your best talents forward in order to get the job done, you'll want to incarnate that inner Tiger. Perhaps the symbolism of Tiger accounts for the mascot chosen by Kellogg's. For decades, Tony the Tiger has been the icon selling Frosted Flakes. After all, which parent doesn't want their kid to be a tiger?

THE MONKEY

In Hebrew, the word for monkey is a variant of the Hebrew word for fun. Monkeys are social, playful, curious, active and fun-loving. Besides being physically and mentally active, they are also, though, labile and unpredictable. They can spontaneously flash into destructive aggression. Perhaps the monkey represents the state of childhood in both its positive and challenging manifestations: youthful exuberance alongside chaotic, unmodulated emotions. If you tend to be very serious, it might do you some good to monkey around a little bit! If your ADHD seems a little *too* monkey-like, better channel some aggressive feline focus!

THE PANTHER

The Panther is a powerful feline, able to leap long distances with a strong jaw and excellent hearing and vision. It's an excellent swimmer, climbs trees effortlessly, but functions best in short, quick bursts of speed. It is solitary and nocturnal, aggressive and protective. Channel Panther when you need to harness aggressive energy and make it work for you to get a project moving forward.

THE GIRAFFE

The giraffe, the world's tallest animal, is a sociable, peaceful plant eater. Giraffes live in herds which function within a hierarchical structure but giraffes do not have bloody power struggles. They do possess sharp hearing and vision and can get by with as little as 5 to 30 minutes of sleep a day. The giraffes characteristic style of moving, slow and elegant, and its height, which could be seen as a metaphor for spirituality, making it a natural stand-in for an important archetype: the temperate wise elder. Giraffes, looking from the higher heights, see the big picture. They see the 'long range'. Further, their distinctive pattern of fur provides excellent camouflage. The giraffe sees all from above but easily hides and avoids detection. When you need the Birdseye view of your life, channel the giraffe.

THE GIRAFFE

THE ROOSTER

Amongst the first prayers of the day in Judaism's liturgy is a prayer of gratitude to the Creator who gave the rooster the ability to discern between day and night. In that tradition, discernment is the most important of human attributes. The rooster, with its intuitive awareness of the forthcoming day, is celebrated. Further, the rooster symbolizes the way we can sense that a new dawn is forthcoming, even when we are shrouded in darkness or dark times. This skill being alluded to is not extrasensory perception. According to the Jewish tradition, the rooster somehow perceives the emergent light within darkness and, therefore, this animal is our role model. We must find the light in the darkness and that helps us to find "the light at the end of the tunnel." Then we can be the person who alerts others to the new, favorable circumstances that surely loom, just around the corner.

THE RABBIT

The signature trait of rabbits, of course, are their patterns of reproduction. Let's think of the rabbit, then, as the archetype of the creative, the one who constantly produces. Such people often have sensitive temperaments. Rabbits are nervous, fearful, skittish, 'jumpy' in nature. The rabbit is prey to various predators and prone to fright. The sensitive artist may be reactive to loud noises or sudden change. Rabbits burrow into the ground where they house their bodies, akin to the sensitive artist who withdraws into his or her lair. Also, since rabbits are social and live in colonies, think of the artist who thrives with an involvement/close relationship with others in the artistic world. Community is important. Also of note: rabbits are most active at dusk and at dawn. Other times, they hang out underground, passing the time. Like the artistic types, rabbits need a certain amount of 'down time'! Literally. When it's time to get productive, that's the moment to channel rabbit! Also when you need to give yourself permission to withdraw and get some grounding!

THE ZEBRA

Zebras are highly social. They don't like to be on their own and will engage with other animals or join other herds to avoid isolation. Zebras have unique stripes that may provide camouflage relative to the animals that prey on them. Yet, each zebra has variance in its stripes. The same stripes that provide camouflage also help individual zebras identify each other. This animal teaches us something about how to retain individuality while also blending into the group.

THE BEAR

Bears take us to the door of paradox. On one hand, they have a crushing bite and stunning strength. Yet, they seem to have a dual nature. Their diet is 90% plant-based. They hibernate in cold weather when food is scarce. Further, our own associations to them are twofold: the violent predator and the teddy bear! Why the dual relationship?

Bears can weigh as much is 1500 pounds yet bear cubs are tiny and require very engaged mothering for a protracted amount of time. Therefore, mother bears are very attached to their cubs and very protective, unleashing violence if their babies are meddled with. The adult is ferocious. The baby is cute. Therefore, we see the Yin and Yang of the bear.

Someone who channels the energy of the bear may be prone to rage . . . and may be a sucker for babies! The brute with a heart of gold!. If you have the temper of a bear, find outlets for the Yin side of your nature! And it's time to bring some gentler animals into the mix!

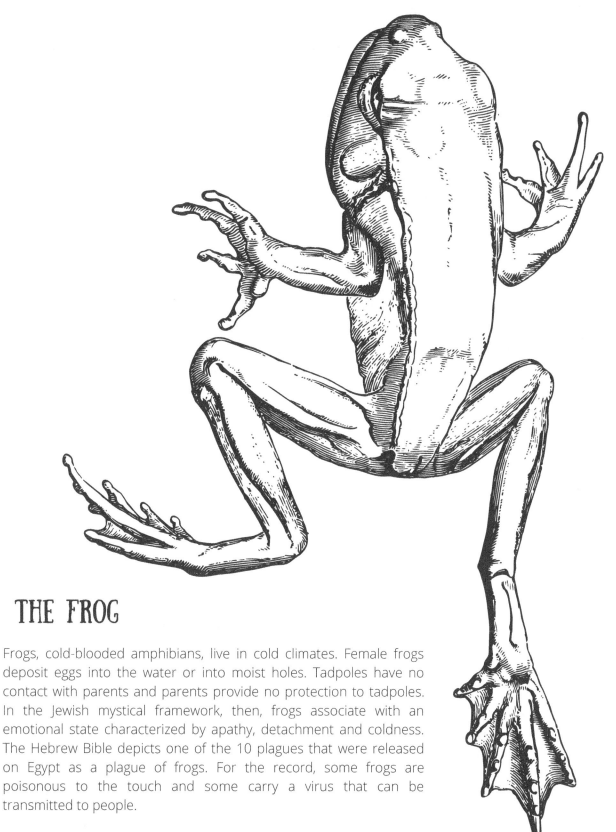

THE FROG

Frogs, cold-blooded amphibians, live in cold climates. Female frogs deposit eggs into the water or into moist holes. Tadpoles have no contact with parents and parents provide no protection to tadpoles. In the Jewish mystical framework, then, frogs associate with an emotional state characterized by apathy, detachment and coldness. The Hebrew Bible depicts one of the 10 plagues that were released on Egypt as a plague of frogs. For the record, some frogs are poisonous to the touch and some carry a virus that can be transmitted to people.

On the other hand, other cultures have very positive associations to frogs. For the Japanese, Chinese or Romans, the frog is a sign of good luck. Perhaps we can think of the fairytale where the frog has the potential, with a kiss, to become the Prince! Of course, North American culture has positive associations, thanks to Kermit the frog!

THE LOBSTER

Psychologist Jordan Peterson finds certain similarities between lobsters and our species but here we want to highlight important differences, especially those that might be instructive or usefully inform the human condition. Lobsters possess hard shells which need to be replaced intermittently to accommodate growth. The process would be akin to a child losing their first teeth and then growing the next set of teeth.

When the lobster's shell becomes tight, the lobster will wriggle out of it. It takes time for the new shell to grow. While this occurs, the vulnerable lobster will retire to a safe space, hiding well away from the path of predators. Defenseless without a shell, a violent wave is all it takes to push that lobster into the path of a passing predator. If the lobster survives the transition phase, though, the lobster regroups and returns to active life in the ocean. From the lobster, then, we learn to release those 'shells' that no longer fit and to allow the phase of retreat, characterized by patience, awaiting new growth and developments. Followers of Jordan Peterson often refer to themselves as lobsters. Many go on to release negative habits and take on new strictures and structures, rules to live by. Indeed, people attempting a reset are often channeling the lobster!

THE COW

Cows are strongly maternal. They nurture each other's calves and, of course, people, as well, by providing dairy. They support humanity in a myriad of ways. As vegetarian animals, they are docile and not a threat. Of course, beef is a food source for some. Even their waste supports us, that being an excellent fertilizer. Their hide is a source of warmth and protection from the elements. It's no wonder that some religions venerate cows ("Holy cow!"). Perhaps this is a status it is accorded because of the good that this animal bestows.

Interestingly, the Hebrew Bible recounts that the Israelites sinned by building and worshiping a golden calf. Is this a message? Perhaps we channel the cow when we activate maternal energy, either by being a giver or an active receiver as we try to access aspects of the world that address our hungers. The golden calf may symbolize the fact that maternal energy can be wrongly manifest. Addictions may exemplify the worship of the golden calf, having us reach for comfortable feelings or states but doing so improperly thereby leading us into excess or vice.

We want to channel this archetype properly and in its healthiest manifestation. We want to reach for healthy forms of nurturance, not those characterized by unhealthy indulgence.

THE PIG

Our use of the English word 'pig' or 'hog' is interesting, bringing us to the idea of excessive consumption. As per the kosher laws, Judaism allows certain animals to be consumed: those with split hooves and those that chew their cud. The pig would deceive us, sporting the outer trait, the split hooves, but not chewing the cud. The pig, therefore represents that which misleads; the outer characteristic tells one story, the inner characteristic, missing as it is, tells the truth. Thinking of the Garden of Eden, Adam and Eve indulged excessively when they were told not to eat, then lied about it. We could argue that the first mistake involved improper and excessive consumption, the next mistake, lying. These are the signature traits we associate with the Pig. As an interesting aside, people who seek endless media coverage are referred to as "media hogs."

To summarize, beyond the excess that we normally associate as the signature trait of the pig, think posturing, acting in order to gain recognition, favor or approval. Perhaps the pig takes us to the address of our own shadow, pointing to areas of excess or indulgence and inviting better calibration as a remedy.

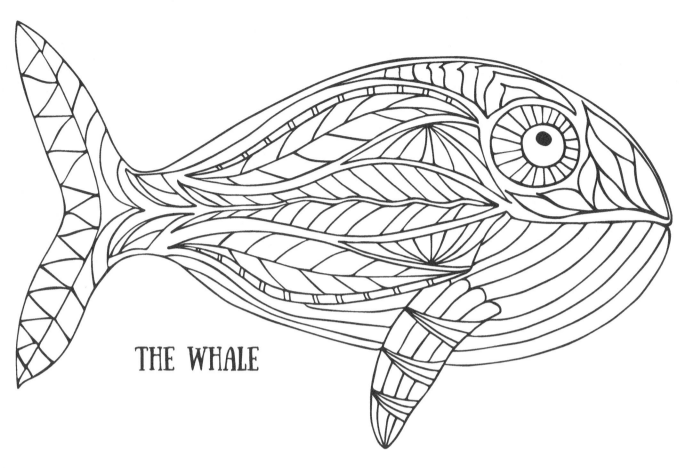

THE WHALE

To understand the whale, we need to consider its context, also its signature traits. Its context is water. Water can remind us of Genesis where we read that the world, prior to an ordering process, is said to be filled with darkness, chaos and void; also covered completely with water. The earth, in that description, consists of nothing but chaotic potential. Water represents something primal, then, perhaps the part of us that is 80% water.

Consider the watery realm as a repository of that which is unconscious and instinctual. Imagine the whale as symbolizing a primal energy that lurks within, the power of one's essence, subsumed in a realm below conscious awareness.

Now think of two signature traits of the whale. Firstly, whales breach. The whale thrusts upward, breaking the surface of the water, launching by leveraging the powerful tail. Secondly: when breathing, the whale forcefully expels air through a blowhole at the top of the head. That air condenses and looks like a stream of water shooting out of the blowhole.

Let's think of the whale as a symbol for the instinctual self which possesses a power that is latent in each person. The task, when dealing with the inner source of essence and intensity, is to find useful outlets, ways of accessing and expressing this aspect of self, not letting it stay hidden, locked within, in the interior realm of potential. we have to breach. We have to push ourselves outward and upward and use that energy, expelling it, expending it and productively expressing it.

Think of the story of Jonah, the prophet given a task to perform. He tries to run away and hide from his responsibility. He takes passage in a ship. Suddenly, a storm rages. It's clear to him that his presence is the cause of the sudden bad weather. He asked to be thrown overboard. The sailors comply and then he is swallowed by a whale. He spends three days in its belly, praying and repenting. Then he is vomited out. He goes on to perform the prophetic task that was his to do.

How do we understand the metaphor of being swallowed by a whale? Our task is to manifest, to expend our core strength and energy in a way that lives true to our destiny and to what the world needs us to achieve. If we resist doing our job, if we lock up our instinctual energy/fail to direct it outward in the way it is meant to be spent, we are not properly channeling this archetype. It's as if we are locked up within the whale. We need to find a way to press forward and move that energy outward, as required. Don't let it be pent up! Don't let it leak in a purposeless and even destructive way. Find healthy ways to express it! The whale should be our power source but it can also be a jail, if we fail to use it properly.

To channel the whale, connect with your reservoir of instinctual energy and find ways to use it productively.

THE SNAKE

Of all the animals, the snake requires a lengthier treatment. Recall the monumental role of the snake in the Genesis 'Garden of Eden' story. Biblical commentators interpret the text, adding a premise that is discussed in the Zohar: when Adam and Eve took their faithful bite from the fruit of the Tree of Knowledge, the snake literally entered their bodies and became a component part of the human psyche. Learning about the snake, then, may take us to certain insights about the shadow; also, the Self.

According to certain commentators, the snake in the Garden of Eden had legs which were removed as a form of punishment for its role in the downfall of humanity. Along these lines, I'm going to suggest the snake represents the psychology of deficiency. Think about it. The snake has no hands, no feet, poor vision, poor hearing. It moves very slowly. It may be without food for months at a time.

Even its upbringing is lowly. Snakes lay eggs and leave the offspring without maternal care. The little snake has to make it on its own. The snake has one long and thin lung. It's cold-blooded and always hungry for opportunities to warm up. The snake has generous access to . . . the dust of the earth. It faces one limitation after another. It only has one advantage: a hinged jaw which allows it to eat prey bigger than its head.

Perhaps with this we see the psychology of the snake, especially as it can play out in our own lives. We all have circumstances which represent challenges or states of deficiency. Financial worries, work problems, the state of the world, social frustrations, health problems, we are all coping with a range of all of these and more. In fact, even in the shape of the snake's body is a symbolic allusion to the world of problems. Think about it. The straight line represents a straightforward path from where we are now to where we want to get. If we can go from here to there without barriers, we are happy. So often in life, though, there are barriers. Imagine that each problem that comes up is like a curve that takes you away from the straightforward acquisition of your goal and now you are needing to accommodate a difficulty. It's going to be a longer and more arduous process. You're going to have to move around that obstacle and somehow figure a way to get yourself back on track. You do and then the next obstacle comes up! Now you have to swerve around that obstacle! And so the shape of the snake is the life course when we are dealing, as we always are, with one problem after another. The question becomes how we will cope with the inevitable barriers we will face.

How does the snake do it? The hinged jaw represents the negative tendency to become consumptive, justifying excess as a means of coping with deficiencies and barriers. If you lapse into this archetype, you may be prone to a victim mentality that, then, opens the door to excess and addictions. Watch for ways you give yourself a free pass to consume endless amounts of sugar, drugs, alcohol, ideologies or other indulgences, all to compensate for the difficulties you are facing. Another form of excess represented by the snake's indulgence: unproductive speech! Remember, some snakes have a venomous tongue! As did the one in the Garden of Eden! Beware the snake that lurks within! And without!

THE OCTOPUS

The eight-limbed octopus, which does not possess a spinal column, is the penultimate symbol of adaptability and flexibility. The octopus can detach limbs and regrow them, another sign of adaptability. Channel the octopus if you need to go with the flow, to multitask, to smoothly move things forward, avoiding conflict while gliding into your best future. In mysticism, the number 8 associates with the ethereal realm, infinite, the zone of magic! Notice that the 8 becomes an infinite sign when you turn it on its side! Flexibility and adaptability are traits that, when we cultivate them, make things work out for us. Magic in action!

"I have treated many hundreds of patients. Among those in the second half of life - that is to say, over 35 - there has not been one whose problem in the last resort was not that of finding a religious outlook on life. It is safe to say that every one of them fell ill because he had lost that which the living religions of every age have given their followers, and none of them has really been healed who did not regain his religious outlook."
— Carl Jung, Modern Man in Search of a Soul

"The development of personality from its germinal state to full consciousness is at once charism and a curse. It's first result is the conscious and unavoidable separation of the single being from the undifferentiated and unconscious herd. This means isolation, and there is no more comforting word for it. Neither family, nor society, nor position can save him from it... The development of personality is a favor that must be paid for dearly.

Carl Jung

"No doubts can exist in the herd; the bigger the crowd the better the truth
– and the greater the catastrophe."
Carl Jung

"We fall captive to the herd animal if we
cannot reach the individual divinity in ourselves."
Carl Jung

" If a man knows more than others, he becomes lonely."
Carl Jung

DREAM JOURNAL

"I HAD A DREAM!"

Use this journal to record dreams you wake up with as you work through the coloring book. Recording your dreams and reviewing them, you may find patterns emerge. Conversely, it is possible that you would need input from an experienced therapist to extract the specific meaning of your dreams. Either way – whether you garner insight from them or not – I'd like to suggest that much is achieved if you record your dreams.

On what basis do I make such a claim?

Let me point out a relevant fact and also a question: why is it that children's fairytales or movies so consistently advance supernatural scenarios? We have talking animals, machines that are alive, magic dragons and the like, just so much unreality. You might even imagine that these storylines are not unlike dreams, full of impossibilities which are presented as normative. Why would children's narratives consistently advance bizarre scenes, by reality standards?

We might get a partial insight if we consider how children acquire immunity. Faced with every germ, every virus, they struggle with each pathogen, ultimately acquiring a capacity, in so doing. Each exposure is a stretch. Similarly, we expose children to many shades of unreality which stretch and tone the imagination. By doing this, the creative imagination will become a conduit to mental health. We frequently assume that the creative disposition is a precursor to madness. But, as GK Chesterton notes

"The madman is not the man who has lost his reason. The madman is the man who was lost everything except his reason . . . . His mind moves in a perfect but narrow circle."

It turns out: rationality is one factor which contributes to mental health. Yet, there are other abilities that must be developed, simultaneously. Rationality allows us to discern and deconstruct reality. Yet, the imagination bench presses in a different way, helping us do important mental machinations. Thinking in all four directions, we can do pirouettes, leaping above and around the limitations of the actual, suspending ourselves in the realm of potential. Also, the imagination can sustain us in bleak moments, reminding us that inner resources can emerge unexpectedly and against all odds, helping us access mythic archetypes that can materialize in a moment's notice. The hero may gallop in and save the day! The elder may emerge with missing information! Miracles happen. The imagination doesn't have to predict the exact right remedy; it sustains us by creating hope and expectation, the implicit faith of transcendent forces which could activate at any moment.

For lack of imagination, a person becomes brittle. This is the person who never dreams. The path of self-exploration, then, requires us to landscape this part of the self. When we do, we develop a faculty that is our bridge to infinity. As Chesterton reflects in his book, *Orthodoxy*, "Poetry is sane because it floats easily in an infinite sea; reason seeks to cross the infinite sea, and so make it finite." The result: mental exhaustion. He adds, "To accept everything is an exercise, to understand everything a strain." Rationality gets us only so far. Imagination does its own version of heavy lifting though achieves this outcome easily, well suited for its job.

And so, you reaching into the irrational world, recording and examining the postcards sent by the active imagination when you awaken, is an elixir. Who said that it is only children who need a steady infusion of the irrational and other-worldly?

We bombard ourselves with the news, constantly reminding ourselves of current limitations. The economy is terrible. People's lives have been devastated by the events of the last two years. No mystery here. And yet, when we have no bridge to the realm of mystery, our troubles are even worse. Chesterton says, "As long as you have mystery you have health; when you destroy mystery you create morbidity. The ordinary man has always been sane because the ordinary man has always been a mystic. He is permitted the twilight. He has always had one foot on earth and the other in fairyland."

Being comfortable with both the tangible and intangible aspects of life, this is the person who can take nourishment from religion. Chesterton says about the one who hosts mystery, He has always left himself free to doubt his Gods; but (unlike

the agnostic of today) free also to believe in them." Not needing to resolve every doubt, able to host complexity and contradiction, Chesterton described this as the person with spiritual sight that is effectively stereoscopic: "he sees two different pictures at once and yet sees all the better for that." He adds:

"it is exactly this balance of apparent contradictions that has been the whole buoyancy of the healthy man. The whole secret of mysticism is this: that man can understand everything by the help of what he does not understand. The morbid logician seeks to make everything lucid, and succeeds in making everything mysterious. The mystic allows one thing to be mysterious, and everything else becomes lucid."

Your dreams, then, are an invitation into the realm of mystery, conjured by the part of self that has a foothold on the irrational. So many years ago, Fritz Perls urged his students to lose their minds and come to their senses. Carl Jung would urge us to loosen the exclusive hold we grant the rational mind and the Persona and to extend a hand to the part that brings offerings from the great beyond. I don't know the shifts you might experience by exerting in this direction – taking an active interest in dreams, writing them down and reviewing them. But I'd like you to find that out for yourself.

CONSIDERING BIBLICAL
ARCHETYPES

UNDERSTANDING BFF'S

On the 50th anniversary of the Mary Tyler Moore Show pilot, we recall the show that put a spotlight on the BFF - 'Best Female Friend' - relationship. Remember beautiful Mary, jealous Rhoda; conventional Mary, quirky Rhoda; beloved Mary, rejected Rhoda. In fact, you find a similar pairing in a more recent show, Grace and Frankie.

If you wondered whether there are classic archetypes at play when we watch a beautiful protagonist and her artistic, less polished, out-of-the-box sidekick, I would tell you 'yes'. Turns out we can learn a lot about ourselves and our friends if we better unpack these prototypes. Who are they? And, further, who are they within us?

Jewish wisdom provides interesting insights. Rabbi YY Jacobson notes that each Torah personality we read about represents an individual that lived but also a timeless characteristic that exists within every human personality. In the case of two sisters who are destined to become wives of the patriarch, Jacob, these two represent two very different distinct aspects of the human psyche.

CONSCIOUS AND UNCONSCIOUS

Leah, the elder sister, corresponds to the unconscious and deeply internal aspects of self, those aspects that necessarily defy expression in words. Jacob was tricked into marrying Leah. She was the rejected wife, deeply sensitive and perceptive, she suffered the ills of the world more acutely, was more subject to tears.

The Torah describes her as having weak or dim eyes. Commentators note that she looked with deep intensity. She had that look of deep apperception, she saw to the core of situations and people. As a result, Leah suffered, she took things to heart.

Rachel, in contrast, was the woman Jacob wanted to marry. The name Rachel derives from the Hebrew word that corresponds to Ewe, a female sheep. Rachel was docile, peaceful, unperturbed. She was beautiful but not complicated. Rachel's gift was expression and mastery of the practical, predictable world. Socially gifted, a character that we easily understand, she is the master of pleasantries and fits in any environment, qualifies for any job, effortlessly masters the tasks the world would have her do. Rachel, we get.

The complicated, brooding Leah, always thinking, always analyzing, lives in a higher dimension. Constantly processing abstractions and values, she doesn't fit into our everyday paradigm. Society is more apt to reject Leah. And to celebrate Rachel.

In the Jewish vernacular, Rachel represents speech and Leah represents thought. Rachel is the master of the 'Revealed world', the social and concrete world, the stuff of everyday life. Leah is in touch with the 'Hidden world', a higher world. She is unconventional, the artist, the musician, the muse. And Leah only finds a home in the revealed world when she partners with Rachel. Hence the prototypical BFF partnership!

It's no coincidence that the Mary Tyler Moore Show centered around a pretty, personable, pleasant Mary Richards. It's no coincidence that Mary produced the news. The Mary in each of us is the speaker, the one who can explain, the one with the basic comprehension of that which is everyday and matter-of-fact. That show presented the Rachel prototype and introduced us to Leah.

Rhoda: brilliantly witty, rough around the edges, blurting out that which most would think but never think to say, coming up with ingenious insights and subject to constant rejection ("Hello. I'm the other person in the room.").

Long-suffering, Rhoda has a difficult time in the revealed world. Everything goes wrong! She doesn't find an easy home here! Or as Rhoda puts it, on the one day when Mary is in a funk and Rhoda is doing well:

"You're having a lousy streak. I happen to be having a terrific streak. Soon the world will be back to normal. Tomorrow you will meet a crown head of Europe and marry. I will have a fat attack, eat 3,000 peanut butter cups, and die."

When Rhoda graduates to her own show, she becomes the Rachel character and her sister, Brenda, is the new Leah, self-deprecating, consistently rejected.

On the other hand, being Leah is not all bad news. Our Leah character is always unabashedly herself. She doesn't succumb to social pressure. Leah represents the zone of internality. Such characters never lose the pulse of their own unique originality.

In contrast, the sages teach, the Rachel character can fall into exile, lose her voice, succumb to social pressure. In the Torah, Rachel represents the *Shechina*, the aspect of Divinity that has been exiled from this world. So the Rachel's of this world have their own problems. Too often, they lose their voice and stray from their truth, often in the context of relationship. They partly find themselves, though, in their pairing with Leah.

And so you have the prototypes: the zany creative and the beautiful ingénue. Each the master of their own domain. The two archetypes work marvelously as a team.

Look around. You'll often see this BFF pairing in the world at large. With every successful partnership, the two domains of the world, the hidden and the revealed, are better bridged. The Mary/Grace character is the master of competence and social convention. The Rhoda/Frankie character brings flavor, insight and novelty into the moment. Rachel is order. Leah has her finger on the pulse of that which is unknown, ephemeral or otherworldly. Leah is 'out there' but her perspective is fresh, interesting and important.

RACHEL AND LEAH WITHIN

Life is full of complexities; for the Rachel's and Leah's in the world; also for the ones we each find, within. The inner Rachel has mastered social mores but sometimes fails to access her own inner truth. The inner Leah houses your idiosyncrasies and aspects of self that are inaccessible, sometimes only channeled through art, poetry or via dreams at night. Rachel is your Sun. Leah is your Moon.

Our first reaction to Leah, whether the one within or the one in the world at large, is rejection. Rabbi Jacobson points out that we hate that which we don't understand. When someone or something is too deep, too incomprehensible, our first response is to deny it or delegitimize it. The inner Leah hosts aspects of the world that are unintelligible, confusing, even overwhelming. Let's put that differently: your Leah hosts aspects of *you* that are unintelligible, confusing, even overwhelming.

And yet, we *must* divine down more complex aspects of reality *and* ourselves. If we will sit with the Leah dimension, reject the urge to turn away, we will befriend imminent aspects of reality (and self) that will expand our lives and our paradigms. We will be better for it.

In fact, the more you integrate your own Leah, the more you can partner with the Leah dimension of your spouse. As Jordan Peterson would say, we have to master the domain of the familiar, but also extend a tendril into the unknown. We have to open to aspects of self and world that don't make sense. We have to figure them out. And escort them into our lives.

You only really get to marry Rachel – and have a life characterized by acceptance – when you marry Leah – first. And so you watch Mary and Rhoda or Frankie and Grace to get a whiff how one might achieve such an inter-inclusion. Watching the social dance between these two archetypes helps us architect and bring together the two prototypes we harbor within.

Long live our BFF's, connecting us to a landscape that is variable and complex, showing us how the other half lives and bringing us into deeper resonance . . . with ourselves!

REFERENCES

Poizner, Annette (2020). *"Knock, Knock": The Kabbalah of Comedy (The How, Why & What of Funny)*. Toronto: People of the Books, Ink.

Poizner, Annette (2020) *Kabbalah Café: Ancient Wisdom for Modern Minds*. Toronto: People of the Books, Ink.

ABOUT THE AUTHOR

Annette Poizner, MSW, Ed.D., RSW

Annette Poizner is a psychotherapist in private practice, a published author and community educator. She completed her Masters degree in Social Work at Columbia University of New York and a Doctorate in Education (specializing in Counseling Psychology) at the University of Toronto.

She has specialized training in techniques developed by Dr. Milton Erickson, as well as advanced training in the use of Eye Movement Desensitization Reprocessing (EMDR) and Neuro Linguistic Programming (NLP). She is the co-founder of the Milton H. Erickson Institute of Toronto. She has a strong interest in Jungian psychology and addresses archetypes within her clinical work with clients.

Her work had been featured in dailies across Canada, in trade magazines across North America, and in clinical and academic venues such as at the Canadian Psychological Association annual conference and other professional meetings. She is the author of a textbook published by a leading scholarly publishing house. "Clinical Graphology: An Interpretive Manual for Mental Health Practitioners." Among her volumes published under the Lobster University Press imprint are: A Practical Summary & Workbook for Using Jordan Peterson's Maps of Meaning to Sort Yourself Out, An Illustrated Guide to Using Jordan Peterson's Insights Regarding Divinity and the Map of Meaning to Sort Yourself Out, In Good Standing: Using Jordan Peterson's Insights on the Structure of Self to Sort Yourself Out, This Way.Up: A Faith-Based Introduction to Jordan Peterson's Maps of Meaning , Clean Your Room: An Out-of-the-Box Manual for Lobsters and From Chaos to Order: A Guide to Jordan Peterson's Worldview. An upcoming volume is Yin, Yang & You: An Eastern Commentary on Jordan Peterson's 12 Rules for Life .

You can access more of her work on her blogs on the Times of Israel and Medium.com and her YouTube channel. To be advised of the release of the next book in this series or to contact her with feedback about this work (which will be sporadically updated) please email ap@annettepoizner.com.

The following pages provide more information about other educational coloring books in this series.

Other Volumes in the Jung@Heart Series:

"The Moon in the Man: A Carl Jung Coloring Book for Self-Exploration"

"Inner Nature: A Carl Jung Coloring Book for Self-Exploration"

"Who am I?"

For many, this most important question goes unaddressed. According to Psychiatrist Carl Jung, people who fail to form a mature, unique identity get lost in pseudo-identities and 'group-think'. Jung warned, "The world will ask you who you are and if you don't know, the world will tell you!" Without the anchor of Self, a person becomes an angry mouthpiece for causes, one more member of the raucous herd.

Annette Poizner, MSW, Ed.D., RSW, a social worker and therapist, has designed workbooks to help readers access Jung's insights into identity and Self. Readers will color images - to improve comprehension, facilitate reflection and also to promote concentration. Accessing Jung's wisdom through summaries, direct quotes and graphic images provides a 'stereophonic' learning experience.

In this volume, readers learn Jung's ideas while coloring mandalas, geometric renderings which Jung felt graphically represented the concept of the Self. As well, when introducing Jung's individuation process, readers unpack the concept through an interesting modality. Poizner, a certified graphologist, shows graphic signs that appear in handwriting, a soft marker that hints at the psycho-spiritual maturity of writers. Signatures of prominent public figures illustrate the phenomenon.

In the next volume, Inner Natures: A Carl Jung Coloring Book for Self-Exploration, we consider why we often reference the animal kingdom when describing people and situations: "I Ie is a real shark!" "There's something fishy going on." "He's a teddy bear!" We will look at animals that embody character traits which play out in our own inner natures and find a range of archetypes represented in the animal kingdom, all archetypes we find within us. Each reader can discover the animal that corresponds to his or her own essence; also each must cultivate traits associated with the wide range of animals. Use this self-reflection exercise to explore the Jungian archetypes and to explore - and expand - your own inner nature.

Learning about Jung's archetypes will spur readers into more active dreaming. The dream journal serves as a log that readers can use to capture their dreams so they can review them over time in an effort to detect patterns.

Part guide, part coloring book, part journal, part mirror, Annette Poizner, a seasoned therapist, has assembled a compelling and personal introduction to the magical world of Carl Jung. In books that that are both educational and experiential, readers can engage in activities which bring Jung's fascinating insights to life.

"Individuation means becoming an 'in-dividual', . . . "individuality" embraces our innermost, last, and incomparable uniqueness . . . "
Carl Jung

Color Me Atomic!
Color Your Way
to Better Habits

Many can benefit from the insights that James Clear has given over in his bestseller, Atomic Habits. BUT not every teenager - addicted to social media and devices - is wont to pick up and engage with a book (you know, objects with multiple pages and writing within). How can we help teens cultivate habits that will see them through, subject, as they are, to rampant ADHD? How do we get them to READ? How do we encourage the development of 'good habits'?

Annette Poizner, MSW, Ed.D., a social worker and therapist, has been drawing young readers to the work of Jordan Peterson and Carl Jung using a coloring book modality. The Jordan Peterson Cheat Sheet, and The Moon in the Man: A Carl Jung Coloring Book for Self-Exploration, are garnering good reviews! Now, Color Me Atomic! is designed to capture the interest of someone you know, providing a compelling introduction to ideas that, when implemented, can be life altering!

Coloring books allow readers to reflect and focus, building concentration skills, this in an age characterized by distraction, busyness and skimming. The coloring book modality is designed to bring quiet back into life. As a modality, it also reinforces what Clear needs us to understand: "All big things come from small beginnings. The seed of every habit is a single, tiny decision."

Want your teen to get back to basics, cultivate patience, and work in a detailed way to audit his or her lifestyle, then implement new habits that can build character and health? Any young person - or old - would do well to color that in!

Once introduced to memorable quotes, concepts and hacks for implementing new habits, readers will find a journal in the back for planning next steps and taking notes when the inevitable (hopefully!) occurs: Clear's book lands on the coffee table, or his audiobook is downloaded on a device!

THE JORDAN PETERSON CHEAT SHEET:
THE COLORING BOOK THAT CAN CHANGE YOUR LIFE!
"A picture tells a thousand words"

Many can benefit from the pearls that Jordan Peterson shares and many have found incredible inspiration in his teachings, but not everyone will tune in to lengthy lectures. If you have been heartened by Peterson's work and looking for a modality that might capture the interest of someone you know, this may be the right gift!

Peterson describes a hallmark of truth, saying "it snaps things together....You have a nature, and when you feel that nature articulated, it's like the act of snapping the puzzle pieces together." In this work, the goal is to facilitate that type of revelation, by pairing compelling quotations with visual images which can then be colored! Using humor, word play and creative visual renderings, this work will unlock insight into self and other, detonating truth bombs that let readers peek into the infrastructure of reality and access some of the fascinating insights that underpin Jordan Peterson's worldview. In a resource designed to inspire growth, learning - and a cleaner room - the author provides an inroad, allowing readers to access teachings that have, to date, catalyzed many.

Coloring books allow readers to reflect and focus, building concentration skills, this in an age characterized by distraction, busyness and skimming. The coloring book modality is designed to bring quiet back into life. As a modality, it also reinforces Peterson's message: 'what if you attended to each detail in your life like it mattered. Imagine what that outcome would look like!'

Once introduced to memorable quotes and concepts, readers can follow up by watching Peterson's lectures. Additional journaling pages are provided for those who further explore Peterson's work to curate content, recording quotes as they come upon them.

Annette Poizner, MSW, Ed.D., is a clinical social worker, therapist and community educator who has written extensively on the work and worldview of Dr. Jordan B. Peterson. Among the books she has written about the work of Jordan Peterson is Finding One Self: A Teenager's Guide to Jordan Peterson's Rules for Life. That book provides young readers with an accessible treatment of many of the rules that Peterson discusses.

Lobster University Press, publishes short volumes which unpack ideas introduced by Dr. Jordan Peterson in his talks and books. The materials published are designed to help people better integrate the material and tweak that most important of abilities: the capacity to "turn chaos into habitable order!" These works will be the product of discourse and exchange with others interested in Peterson's work, as we continue to mine the depth of his opus and explore interesting and helpful applications.

Lobster University Press

"Finding One Self: A Teenager's Guide to Jordan Peterson's Rules for Life

Countless young men have been helped by the ideas of Canadian psychologist Jordan Peterson. The question remains: does this eminent psychologist's opus of work have something to offer young women?

Annette Poizner suggests it does: young women will be fascinated to learn about the map of meaning that they harbor within, a map that the unconscious mind builds to manage chaos, an inherent part of reality. In this book, readers access a summary of some of the 'rules for life' they can implement to mastermind their best self & enhance self-image; rules which provide an anchor, in the face of today's normlessness.

Drawing on decades of clinical experience, Poizner speaks directly to young women, tailoring the rules to a reality heavy on electronics, light on consensus. Short chapters provide usable soundbites. Readers walk away with strategies to make changes and get a personalized introduction to Dr. Peterson's work, designed for those new to some ideas that have taken the world by storm!

Made in the USA
Middletown, DE
17 November 2023

42963294R00080